MY BASEBALL FAN CAN WRITE!

Trace, Color & Draw Me

THIS BOOK BELONGS TO:

People learn from trial and errors, Mistakes happen, Learn from them and make it better!

ARTWORK

Erase and practice
as many times as
you want.

ARTWORK

Please bring an
extra pencil
and
an eraser too

ARTWORK

Please sharpen your pencil and let's begin!

ARTWORK

Directions

Let's start with the Alphabet, trace the letters and then words.

ARTWORK

Eraser, Eraser
Where are you?
Here I am,
Here I am!

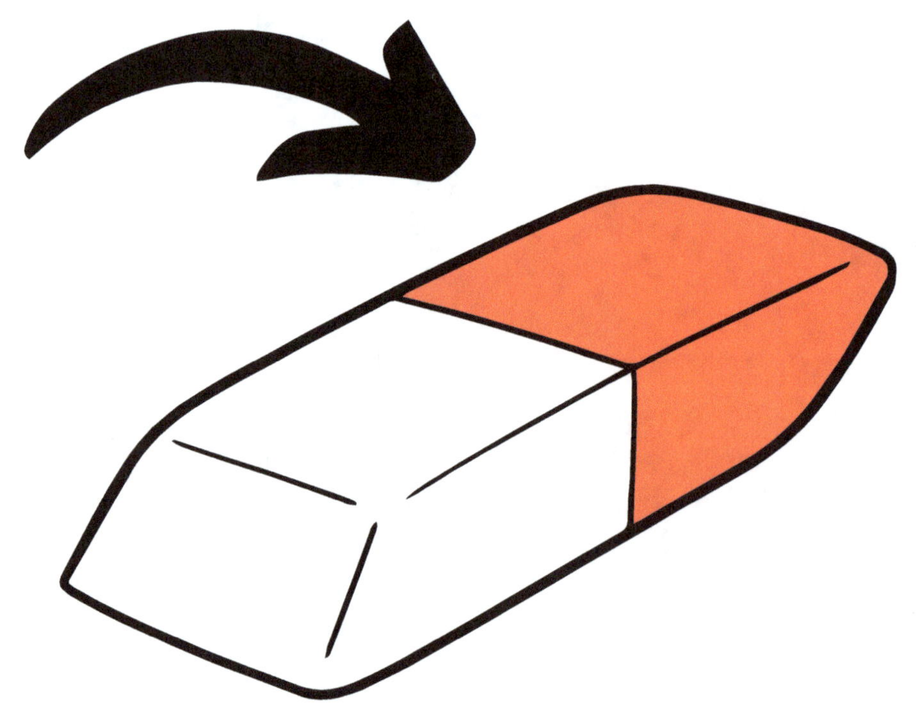

ARTWORK

A is for Apple

Trace Me:

APPLE

apple

Color Me:

Draw Me:

ARTWORK

Bb

B is for Basket

Trace Me:

BASKET

basket

Color Me:

Draw Me:

ARTWORK

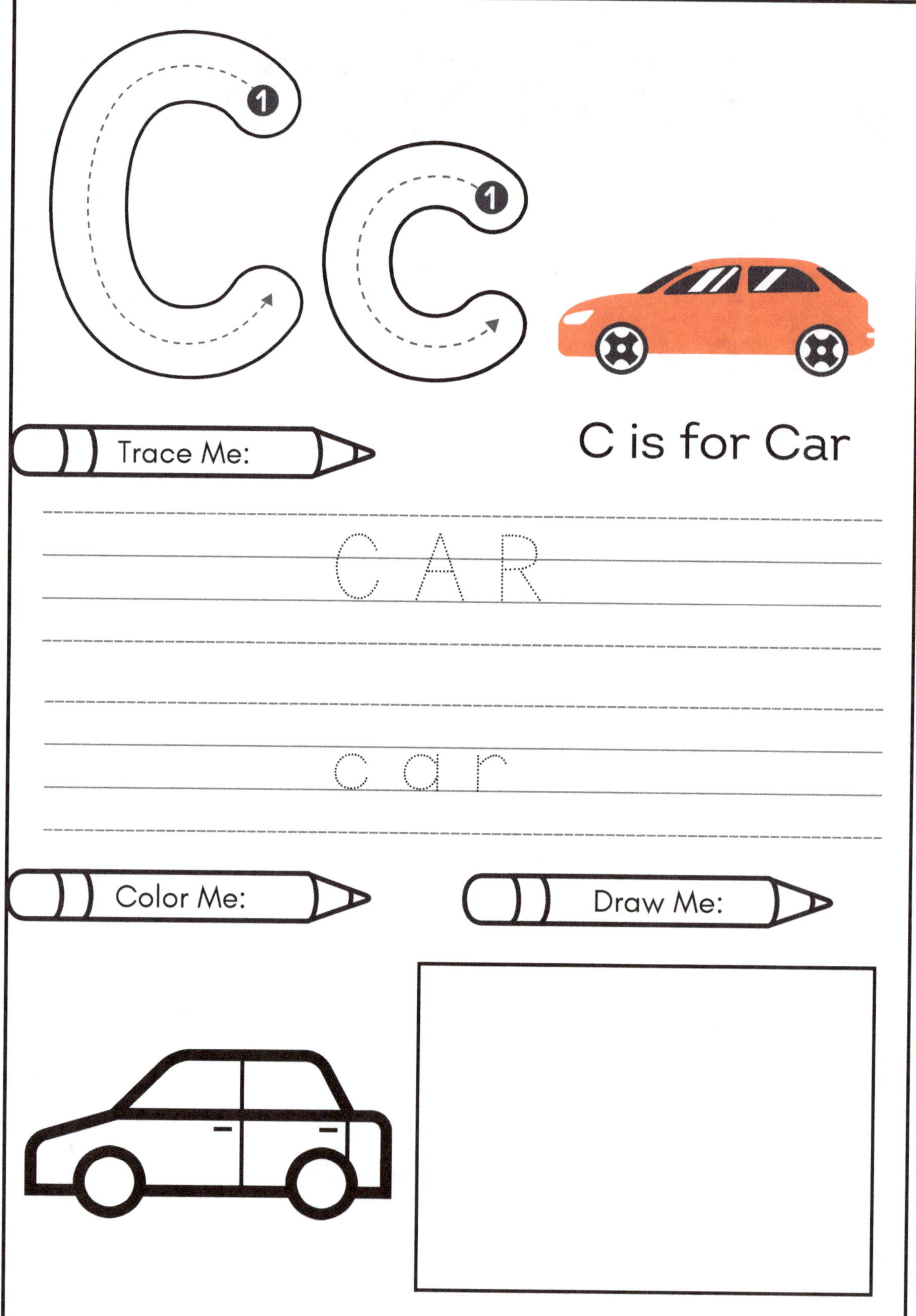

C is for Car
Trace Me:
CAR
car
Color Me:
Draw Me:

ARTWORK

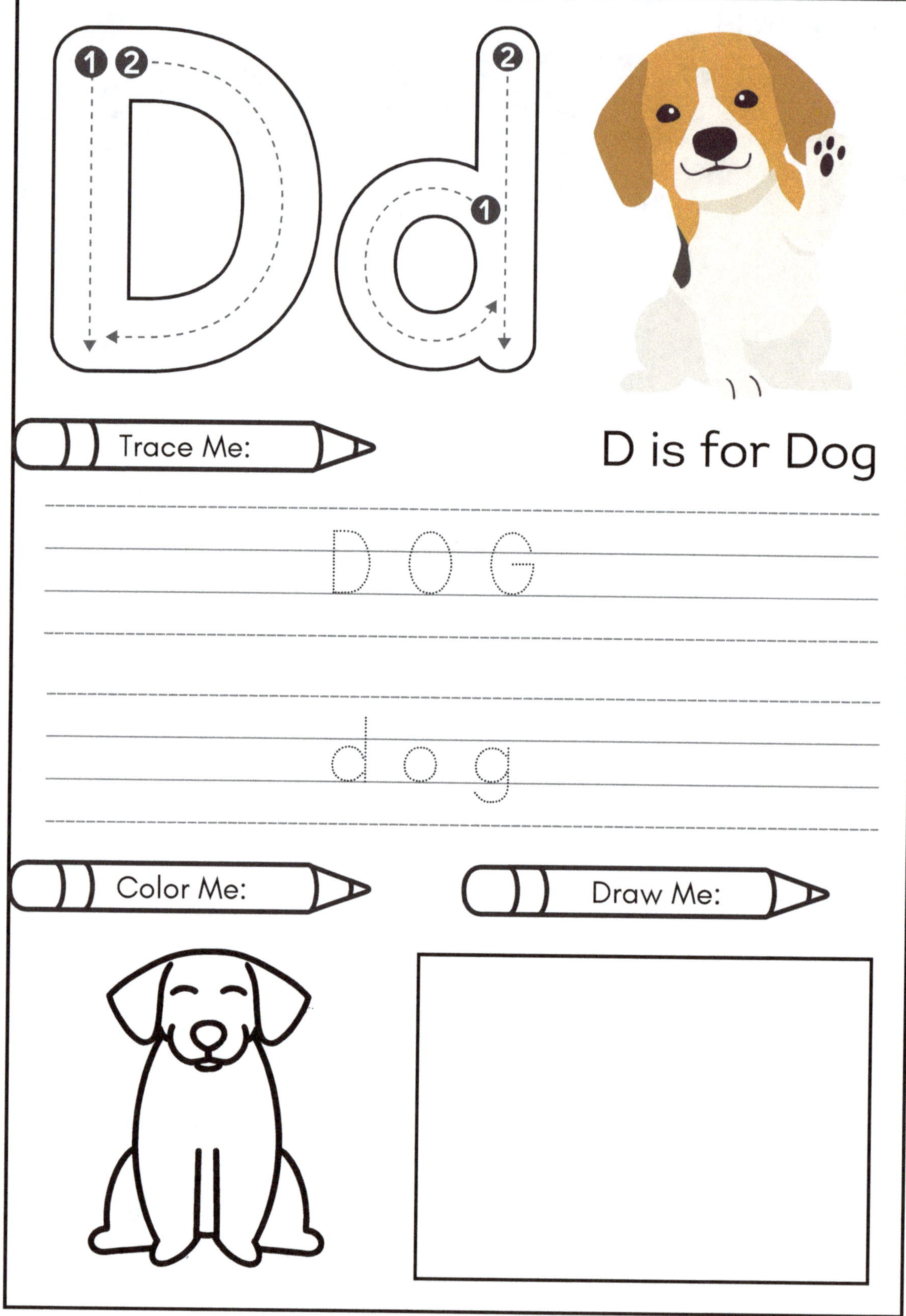

D d
Trace Me:
D is for Dog
D O G
d o g
Color Me:
Draw Me:

ARTWORK

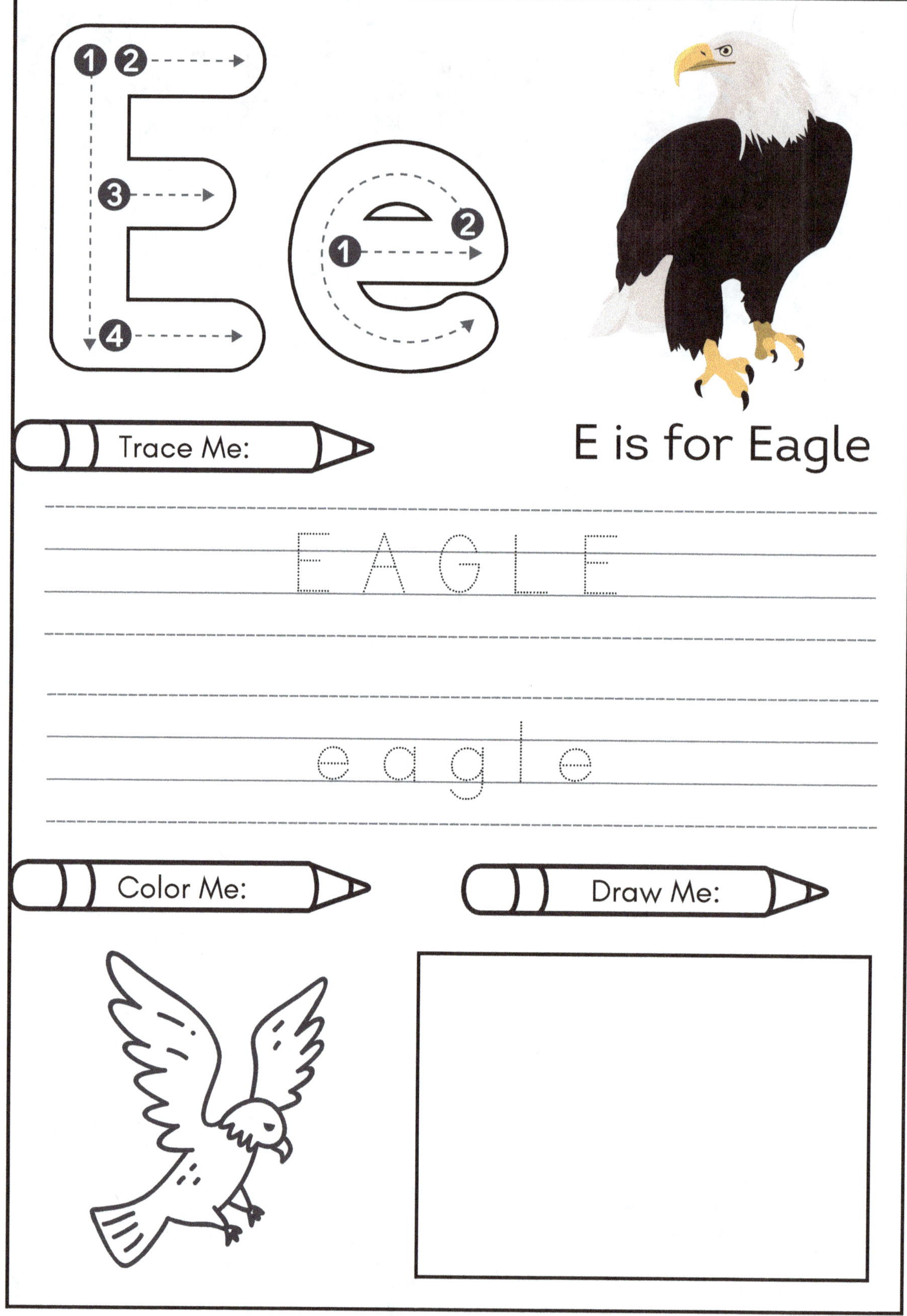

Trace Me:
E is for Eagle
EAGLE
eagle
Color Me:
Draw Me:

ARTWORK

F is for Fish
Trace Me:
FISH
fish
Color Me:
Draw Me:

ARTWORK

G is for Goat

Trace Me:

G O A T

g o a t

Color Me:

Draw Me:

ARTWORK

Hh
Trace Me:
H is for Heart
HEART
heart
Color Me:
Draw Me:

ARTWORK 

I is for Igloo

Trace Me:

IGLOO

igloo

Color Me:

Draw Me:

ARTWORK

J is for Jar

Trace Me:

JAR

jar

Color Me:

Draw Me:

ARTWORK

K k

K is for Kangaroo

Trace Me:

KANGAROO

Kangaroo

Color Me:

Draw Me:

ARTWORK

1
1
2
L is for Lion
Trace Me:
L I O N
l i o n
Color Me:
Draw Me:

ARTWORK

M m
M is for Money
Trace Me:
MONEY
money
Color Me:
Draw Me:

ARTWORK

N n
Trace Me:
N is for Nuts
N U T S
n u t s
Color Me:
Draw Me:

ARTWORK

O is for Onion

Trace Me:

O N I O N

o n i o n

Color Me:

Draw Me:

ARTWORK

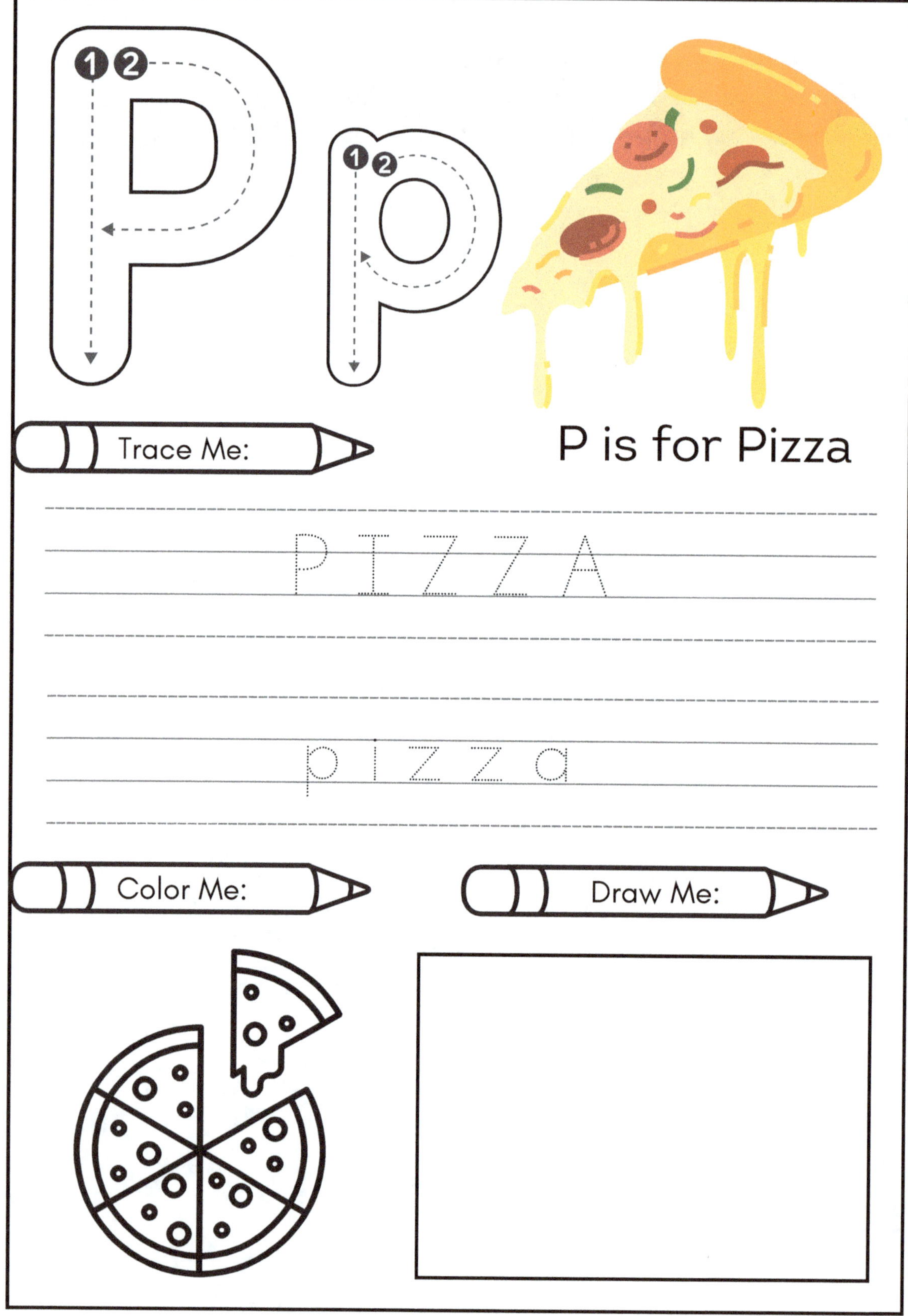

P
p
P is for Pizza
Trace Me:
PIZZA
pizza
Color Me:
Draw Me:

ARTWORK

Q is for Quail

Trace Me:

QUAIL

quail

Color Me:

Draw Me:

ARTWORK

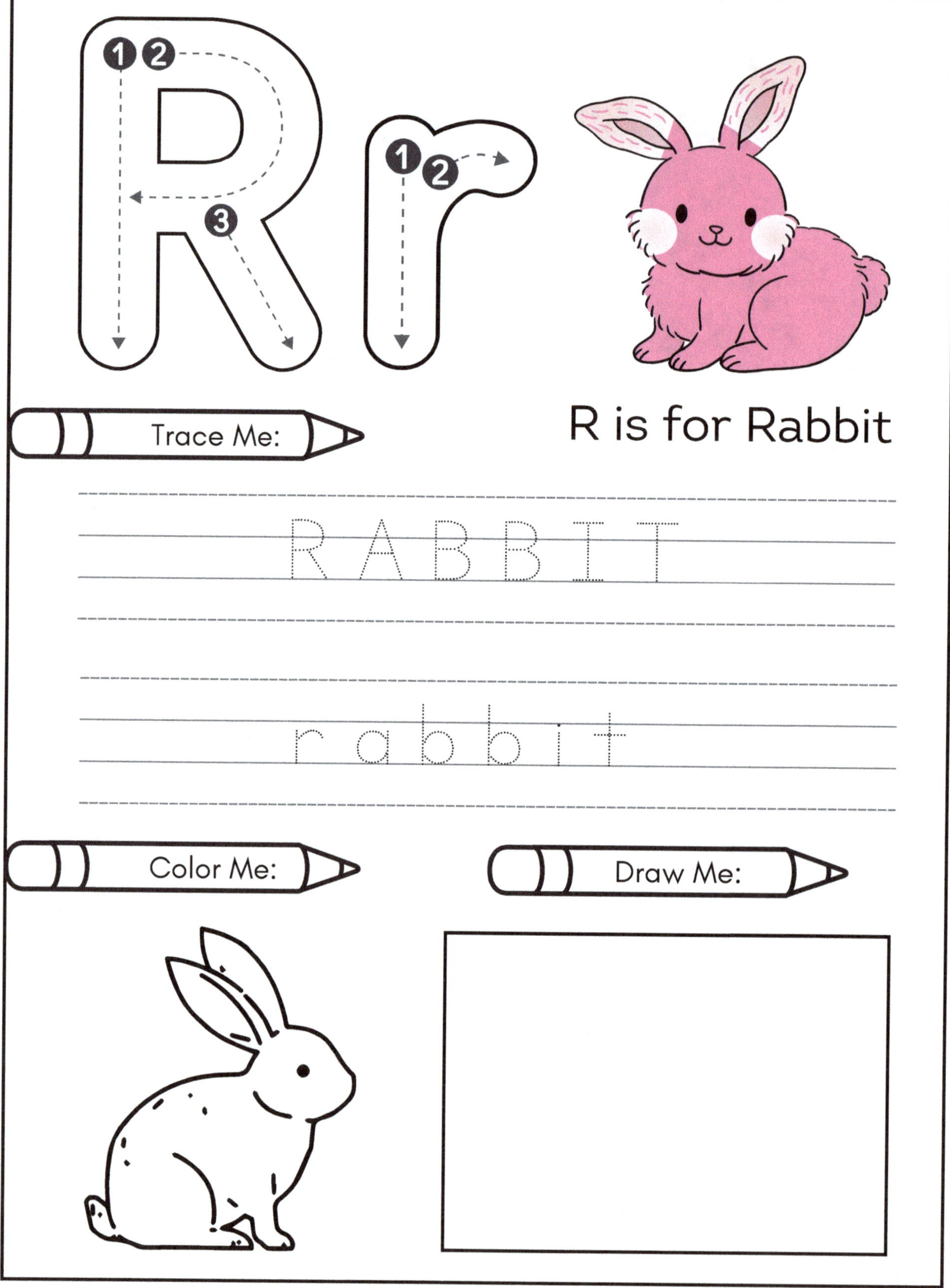

R is for Rabbit

Trace Me:

RABBIT

rabbit

Color Me:

Draw Me:

ARTWORK

S is for Sun

Trace Me:

S U N

s u n

Color Me:

Draw Me:

ARTWORK

T is for Tree

Trace Me:

TREE

tree

Color Me:

Draw Me:

ARTWORK

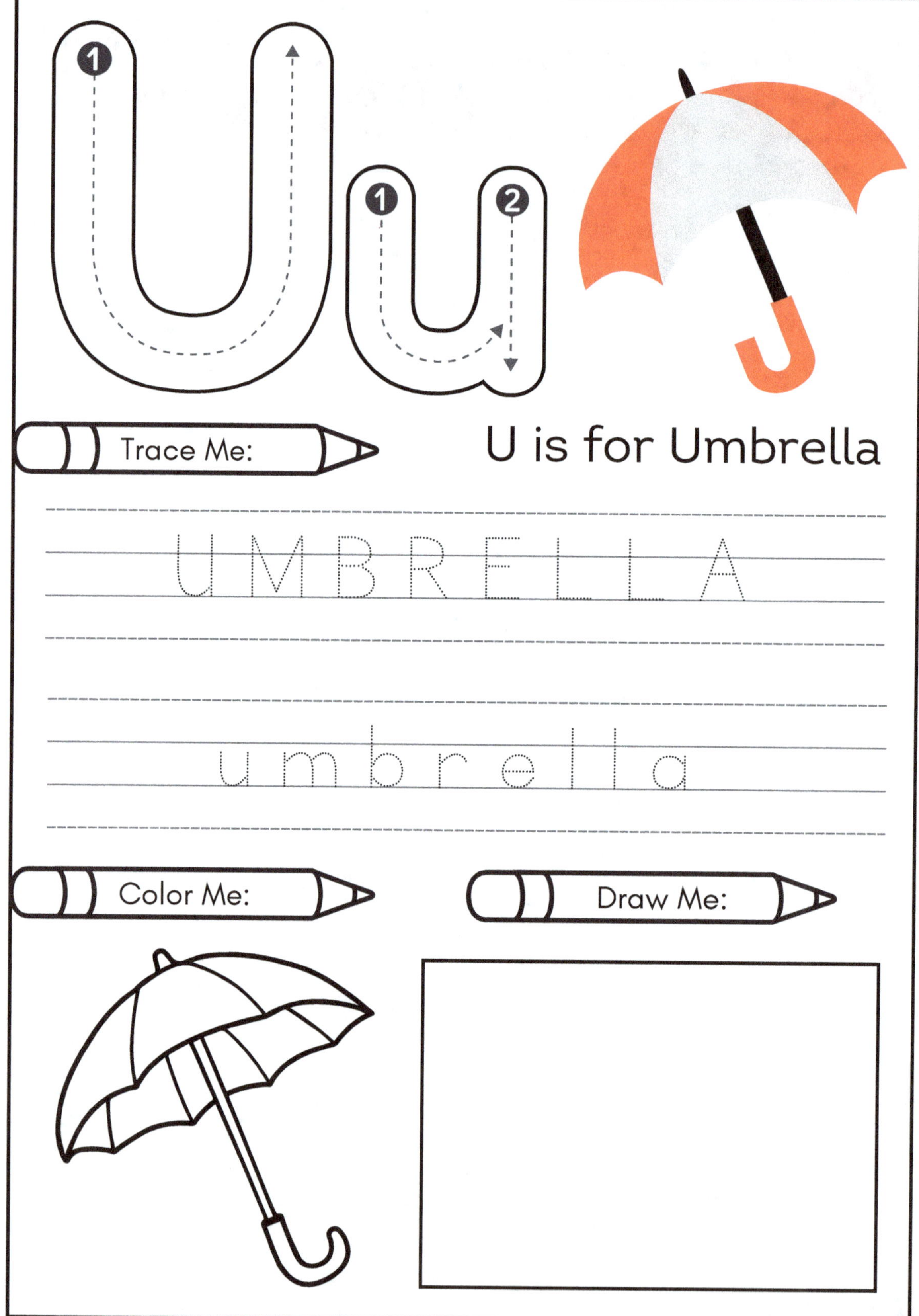

U is for Umbrella

Trace Me:

U M B R E L L A

umbrella

Color Me:

Draw Me:

ARTWORK

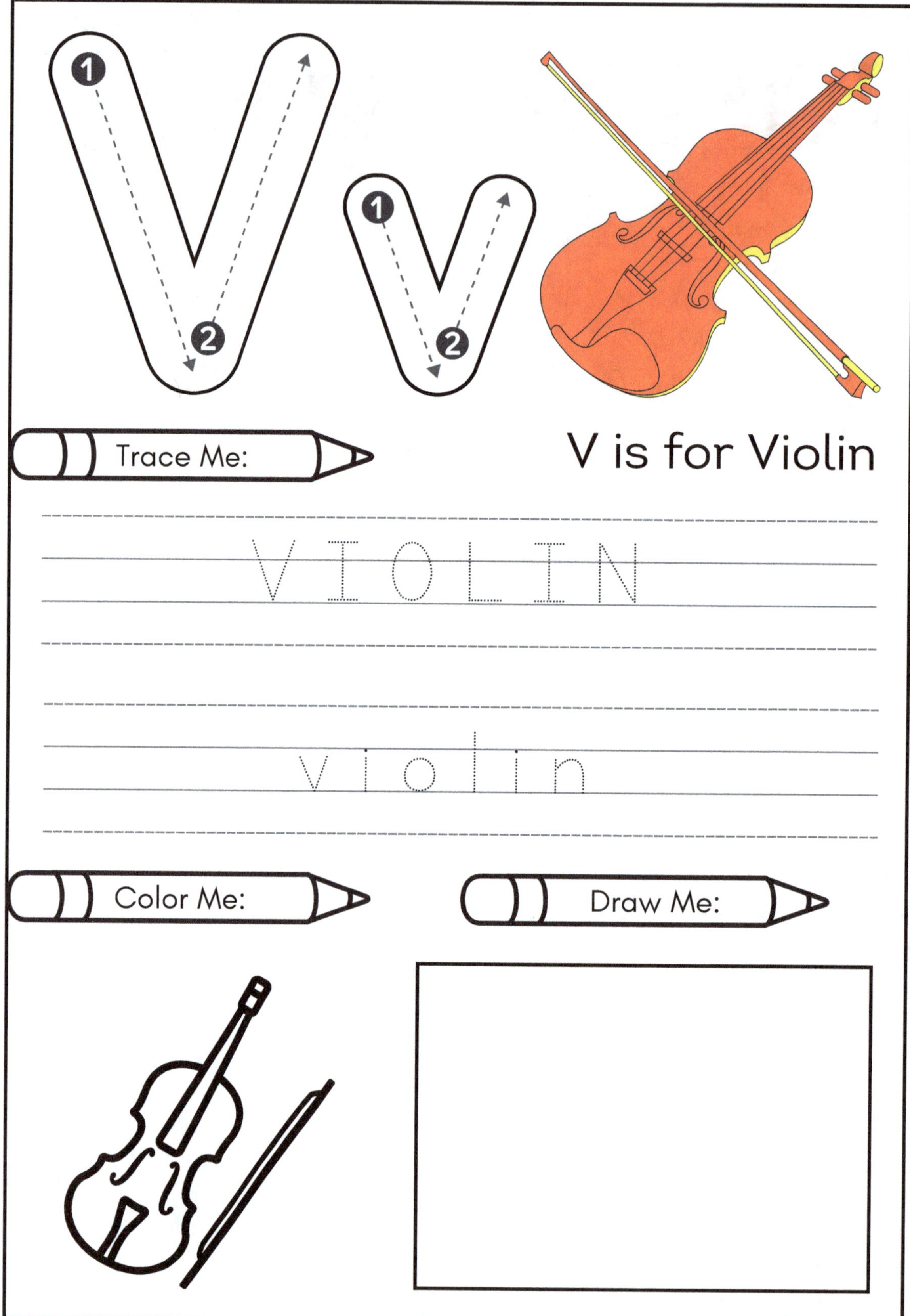

Trace Me:

VIOLIN

violin

Color Me:

Draw Me:

V is for Violin

ARTWORK

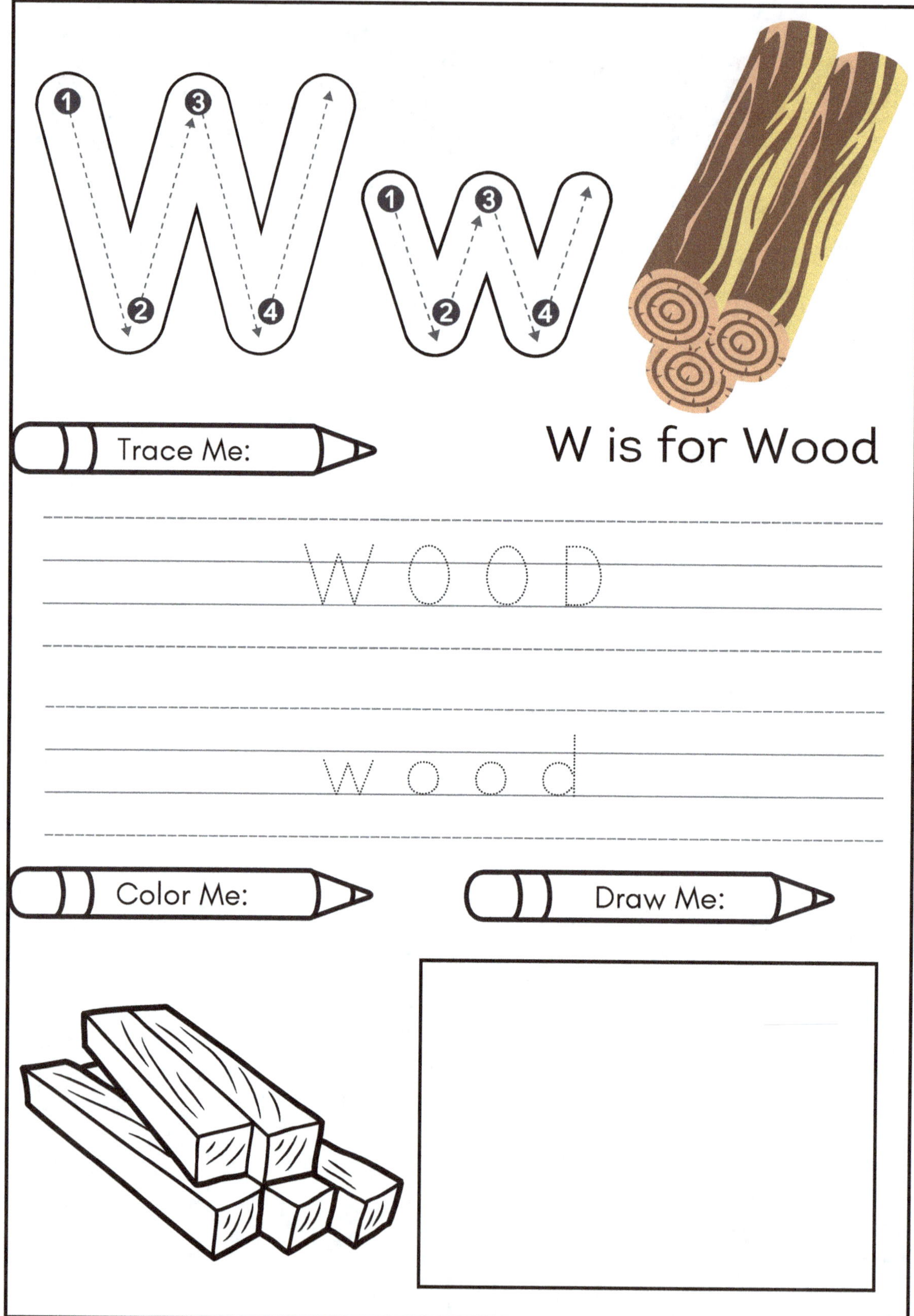

W is for Wood

Trace Me:

W O O D

w o o d

Color Me:

Draw Me:

ARTWORK

X is for Xylophone

Trace Me:

XYLOPHONE

xylophone

Color Me:

Draw Me:

ARTWORK

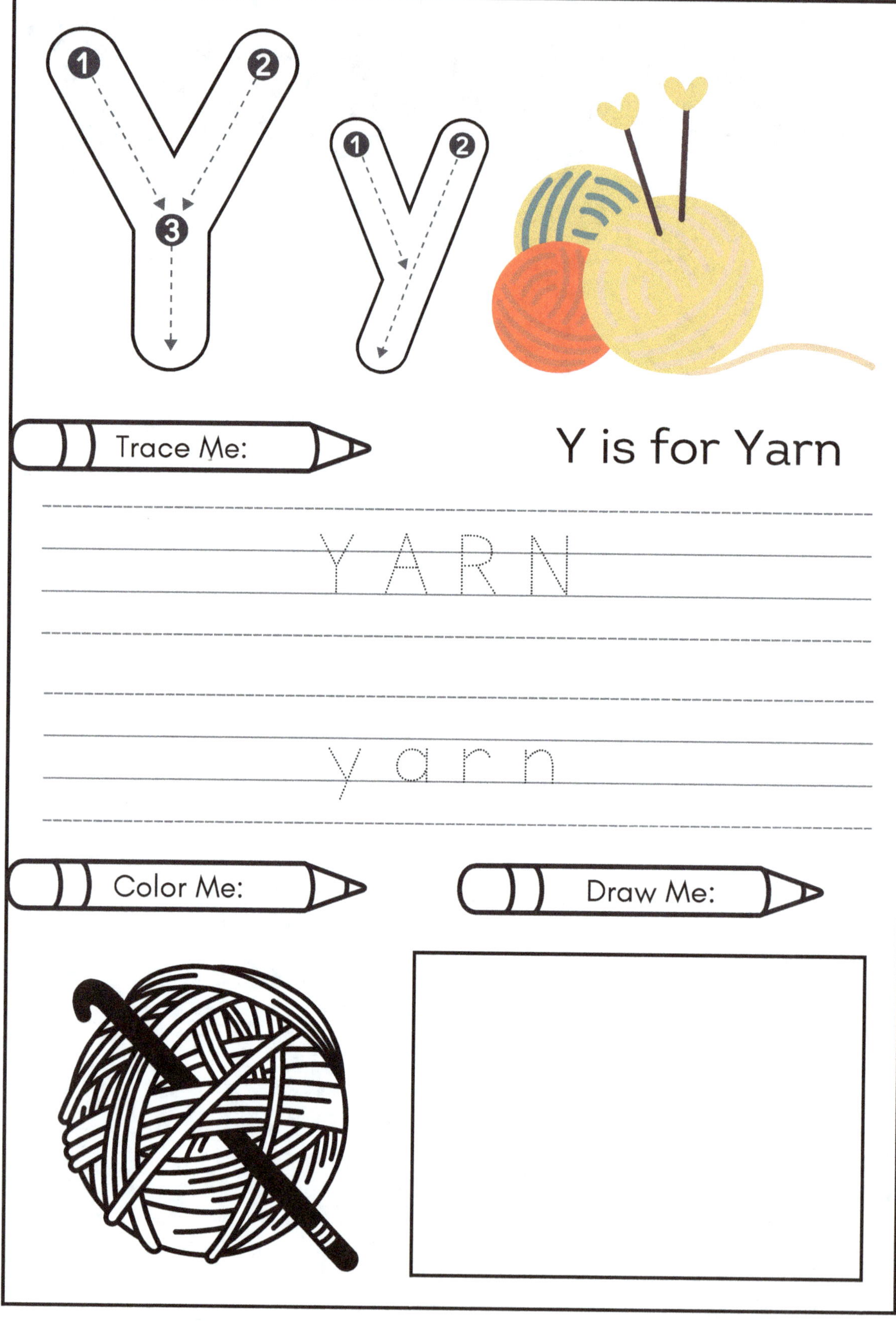

1
2
3
Trace Me:
Y is for Yarn
YARN
yarn
Color Me:
Draw Me:

ARTWORK

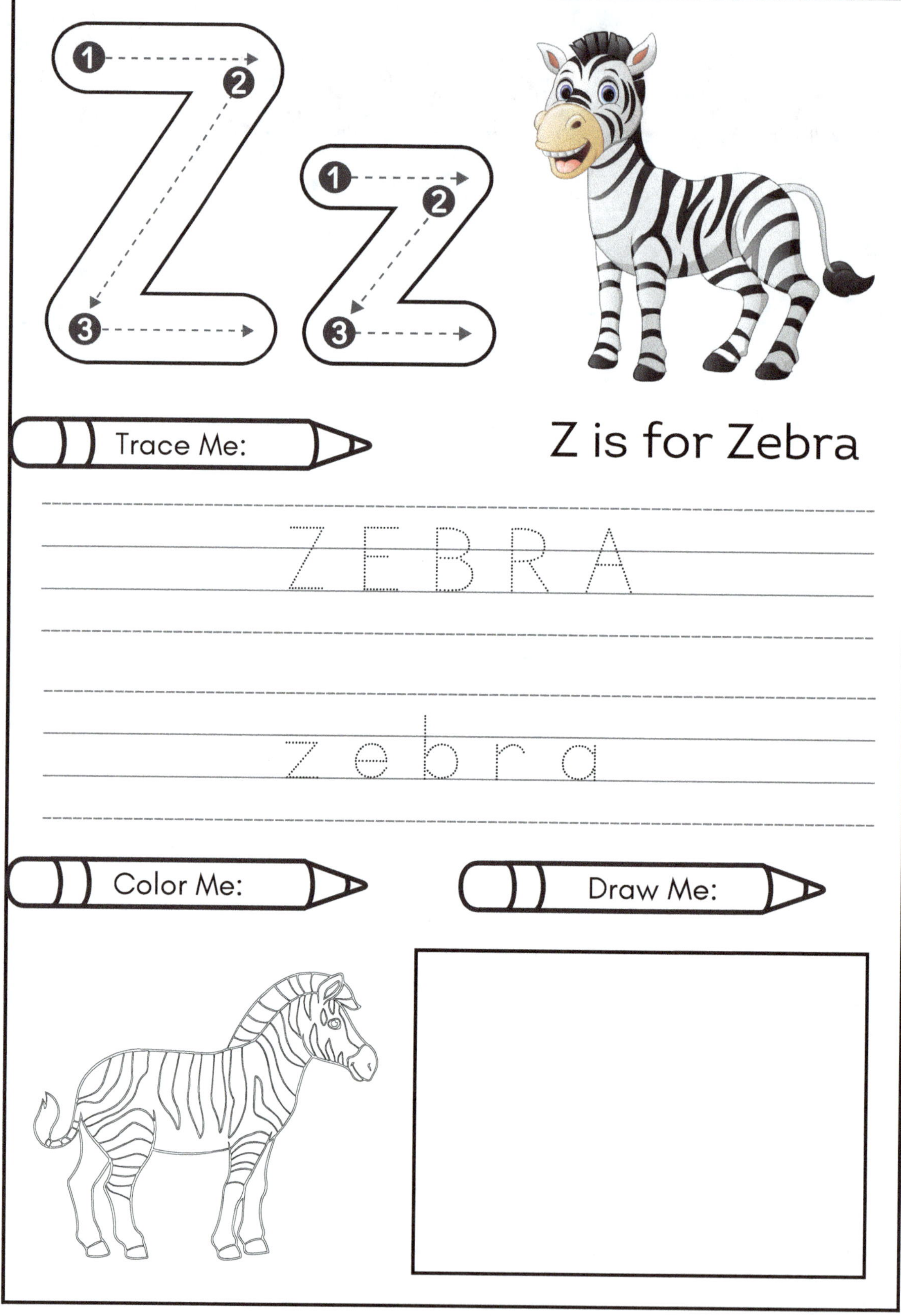

1
2
3
1
2
3
Z is for Zebra
Trace Me:
ZEBRA
zebra
Color Me:
Draw Me:

ARTWORK

Great News!

My Baseball

Fan can write!

ARTWORK

COUNT & COLOR ME 

Can my Baseball
Fan count?

1

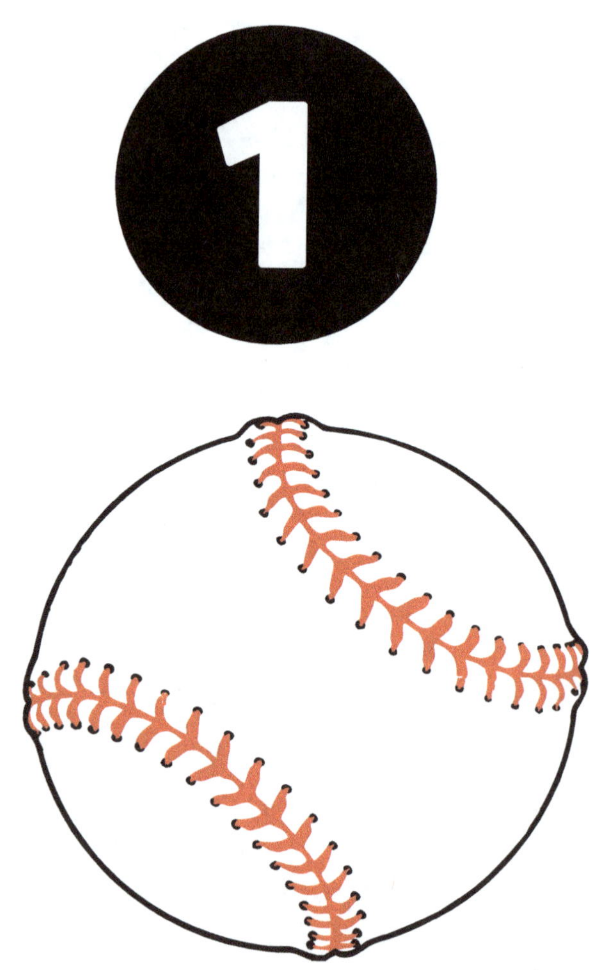

ARTWORK

COUNT & COLOR ME 

2

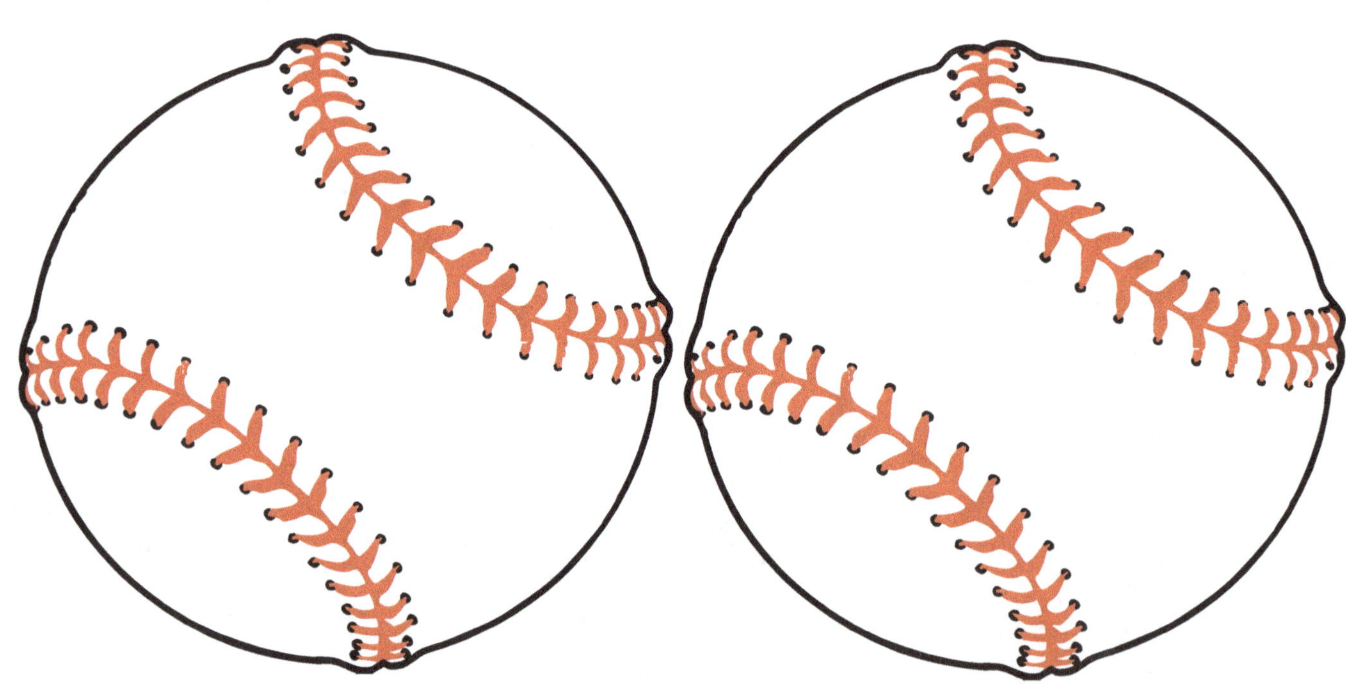

ARTWORK

COUNT & COLOR ME 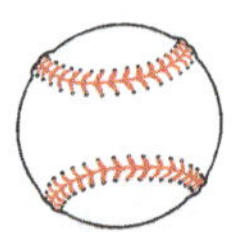

3

ARTWORK

COUNT & COLOR ME 

4

ARTWORK 

COUNT & COLOR ME 

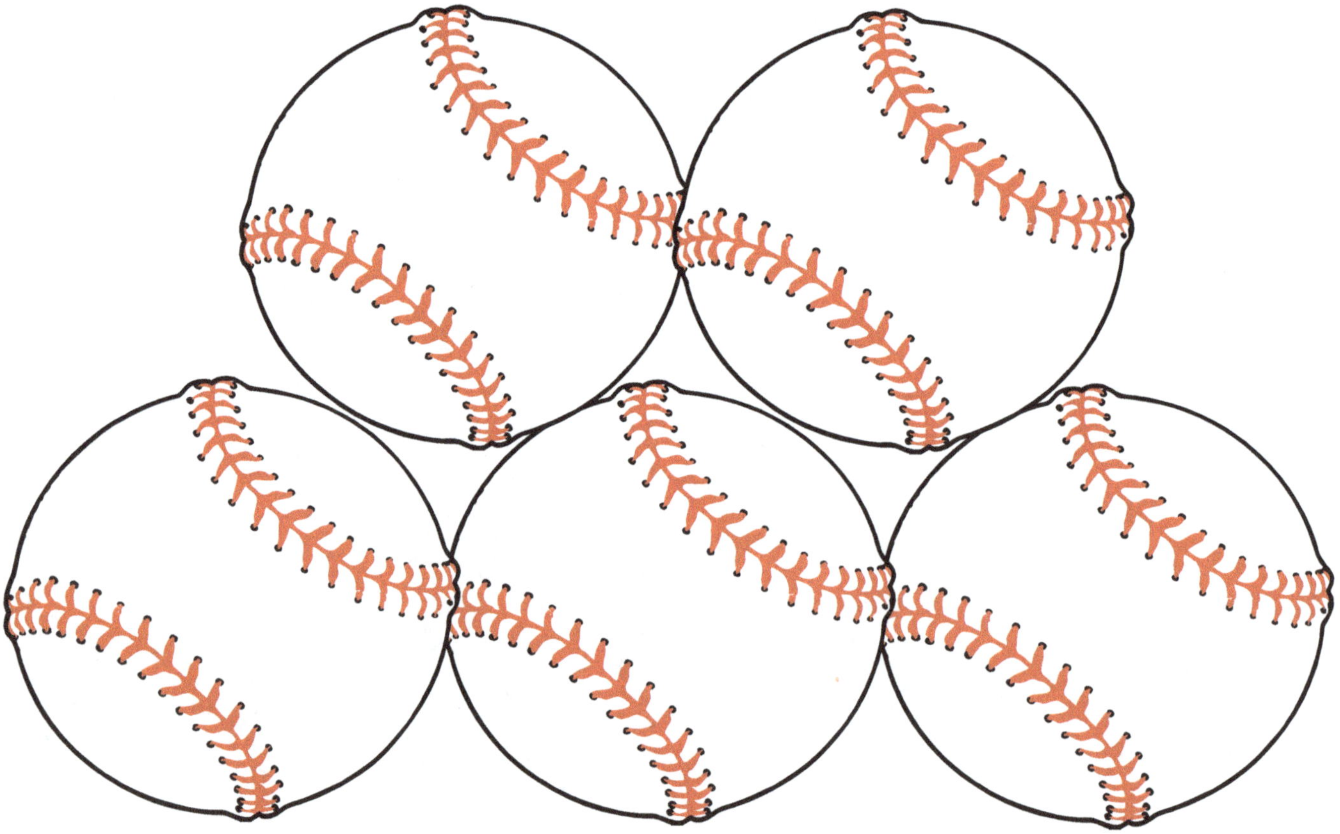

ARTWORK

COUNT & COLOR ME 

6

ARTWORK 

1-2-3-
IT'S A HOME RUN!